CRUSHING
CHAOS
STUDY GUIDE

T0356686

CRUSHING CHAOS STUDY GUIDE

Calm Your Storms.
Order Your Life.
Find Your Peace.

Manny Arango

WATERBROOK

WaterBrook
An imprint of the Penguin Random House Christian Publishing Group,
a division of Penguin Random House LLC
1745 Broadway, New York, NY 10019
waterbrookmultnomah.com
penguinrandomhouse.com

A WaterBrook Trade Paperback Original

Copyright © 2025 by Manny Arango Ministries, Inc.

Penguin Random House values and supports copyright. Copyright fuels creativity,
encourages diverse voices, promotes free speech, and creates a vibrant culture. Thank you
for buying an authorized edition of this book and for complying with copyright laws by
not reproducing, scanning, or distributing any part of it in any form without permission.
You are supporting writers and allowing Penguin Random House to continue to publish
books for every reader. Please note that no part of this book may be used or reproduced in
any manner for the purpose of training artificial intelligence technologies or systems.

WATERBROOK and colophon are registered trademarks of Penguin Random House LLC.

Interior illustration: @ Spencer Fuller/Faceout Studio (dragon)

Some material is adapted from *Crushing Chaos* by Manny Arango, copyright © 2025 by
Manny Arango Ministries, Inc., published in the United States by WaterBrook, an imprint
of the Penguin Random House Christian Publishing Group, a division of Penguin
Random House LLC, in 2025.

Library of Congress Cataloging-in-Publication Data

Names: Arango, Manny, author.
Title: Crushing chaos study guide : calm your storms. order your life. find your peace. /
Manny Arango.
Description: [Colorado Springs, CO] : WaterBrook, [2025]
Identifiers: LCCN 2024043184 | ISBN 9780593601631 (trade paperback) |
ISBN 9780593601648 (ebook)
Subjects: LCSH: Christian life—Study and teaching. | Chaos (Christian theology)
Classification: LCC BV4509.5 .A735 2025 | DDC 248.4—dc23/eng/20241209
LC record available at https://lccn.loc.gov/2024043184

Printed in the United States of America on acid-free paper

9 8 7 6 5 4 3 2 1

The authorized representative in the EU for product safety and compliance is Penguin
Random House Ireland, Morrison Chambers, 32 Nassau Street, Dublin D02 YH68,
Ireland. https://eu-contact.penguin.ie

BOOK TEAM: Production editor: Jessica Choi • Managing editor: Julia Wallace • Production
manager: Maggie Hart • Copy editor: Tracey Moore • Proofreaders: Marissa Earl, Carrie
Krause

Book design by Diane Hobbing

For details on special quantity discounts for bulk purchases, contact
specialmarketscms@penguinrandomhouse.com.

Contents

SESSION 4   COME HELL OR HIGH WATER

SESSION 5   THE PRINCE OF PEACE: FIRST HALF

SESSION 6   THE PRINCE OF PEACE: SECOND HALF

How to Use This Guide

Hey,

I'm glad you're here. Reaching out to you through these pages is a privilege. And I prayed for you as I wrote. Consider this an invitation to pray for me, too, as you read—I need it!

This is a six-week study of *Crushing Chaos*. You'll be reading through the book on your own and discussing it with a group. I've set it up so the guide is split into six sessions, and each session has work for you to do yourself—On Your Own—before your group then meets—All Together.

Here's the rhythm: Read the content for yourself, wrestling with it as you go, then gather as a group and take your understanding to the next level. There are three to seven chapters for each session—that's no more than a chapter a day of reading if you're meeting once a week. But I know that some readers will do all the work in one day, while others of you will spread the reading out over the whole week. I'm not here to judge—I want you to make this time of study your own.

On Your Own

The On Your Own portion of each session is split into three parts:

Before You Read	While You Read	After You Read
A guided reflection from me to prepare you for the chapters	Your own notes on scripture, insights from and questions about the text, and quotes of significance to you	A space to prepare your thoughts and questions for the group

All Together

The All Together portion will be a time for your group to dive deeply into the scripture and chapter themes through group discussion and prayer. A huge feature of the group discussion will be the thoughts and questions you come up with during your own reading.

Here's the overview of the chapters for each session:

Session 1 A World of Chaos: First Half	Session 2 A World of Chaos: Second Half	Session 3 Taming the Beast	Session 4 Come Hell or High Water	Session 5 The Prince of Peace: First Half	Session 6 The Prince of Peace: Second Half
Chapters 1–4	Chapters 5–7	Chapters 8–13	Chapters 14–20	Chapters 21–24	Chapters 25–29

I can't wait to introduce you to the Chaos-crushing God of the Bible. There's a whole world for us to discover and a totally, radically new way to see it. Let's do this together.

CRUSHING
CHAOS
STUDY GUIDE

A WORLD OF CHAOS: FIRST HALF

On Your Own

Before You Read

You don't have to look very far to find chaos. The word *chaos* means "a state of complete confusion and lack of order."* Generally speaking, chaos is the reality that all is not well, that things are not right. You've felt chaos before. If I asked what you think the most chaotic thing happening in the world today is, you'd probably have trouble

---

* *Oxford Learner's Dictionaries,* "chaos," accessed October 28, 2024, www.oxfordlearnersdictionaries.com/us/definition/american_english/chaos.

choosing just one. If I asked about the most chaotic thing that happened to you last week, I know you'd have a story for me.

Chaos is everywhere—in our world and in us.

This week, we're exploring a story that you've heard and read before. Even if you don't think you've heard it, I'll bet you probably have. But I want you to hear it differently this time. I want you to notice something new.

So, before we get started, what do you remember about the creation story? Don't look at your Bible—not yet, at any rate. I just want you to remember what you've heard. I'll help you start: In the beginning . . .

_____

_____

_____

_____

_____

So, what is the creation story about? I want to know what you think before we get into it together. Why is this story in the Bible? Why does Scripture start here? What are we supposed to be learning?

_____

_____

Now, open a Bible. Any Bible. It's right there at the beginning—Genesis 1. Take a deep breath, and quiet your heart and mind. Read through the verses slowly.

Where's the Chaos in the creation story? And what did God decide to do about it?

That's what these first chapters are about.

While You Read

Use these pages to take notes as you read each chapter. There are no right or wrong answers. If making an outline helps you focus, do that. If you want to pay special attention to definitions, to write questions about things that confuse you, or to write out why you disagree with me, do that.

In case you need some motivation, here's what I've got: Reading the content ahead of time and taking a few notes is a great way to prepare some thoughts for anyone else you're studying with. Maybe someone needs to ponder the question or hear the insight you're going to think of as you're reading. You're not just doing this for yourself.

So, while you read, have this study guide nearby. For each chapter, I want you to do these three things:

1. Make a note of any scripture in the chapter that stands out to you. Mark significant passages in your Bible.
2. Write a few thoughts inspired by the chapter, or copy a few phrases that are significant to you. I'm talking about phrases that make you stop and think, phrases that inspire wonder, ideas that confuse you, and even things that make you angry or that you totally disagree with. You can copy them straight from the book or use your own words. This is your space to interact with the chapter—make it your own.
3. Finally, summarize your experience of the chapter, writing out a thought, question, or insight in the space marked "I want to remember . . ." Think of this as the one thing you want to make sure to bring to your group.

Chapter 1

Panic in the Lobby

> Creation was a . . . barren, unintelligible, chaotic
> ocean abyss. . . . However, God didn't bring
> peace to this chaos. God began organizing the
> creation and moved the earth from chaos into
> *order*. God began to separate, pull apart, gather,
> and bring structure to the chaos of creation.
> (page 4)

Scripture in This Chapter

Genesis 1:1–2, 6–7, 9   Galatians 5:22–23
Matthew 13:23   Genesis 2:7

Thoughts, Insights, Questions

_____

_____

_____

_____

_____

I want to remember . . .

_____

_____

_____

Chapter 2

Peace in the Temple

Ancient audiences understood that deities rested only once their temples were ordered and sanctified. Rest was the final confirmation that the space was sacred. Rest was synonymous with divine approval. . . . In the ancient world, gods rested only in temples, nowhere else. Because *where* you rest will dictate *how* you rest. (pages 13–14)

Scripture in This Chapter

Genesis 2:2	Judges 16:19
Matthew 11:28	John 2:19–21
Genesis 1:26	1 Corinthians 6:19–20
Genesis 4:11–14	Genesis 3:8

Thoughts, Insights, Questions

_____

_____

_____

_____

_____

I want to remember . . .

_____

_____

_____

Chapter 3

Monsters in the Bible

Yahweh never calls anything in the creation narrative perfect; He calls everything He made good. Everything. No exceptions. That includes the tree of the knowledge of good and evil. And the crafty Serpent. And the fruit that Adam and Eve are forbidden to eat.

This is a curveball. There are elements of Chaos residing in God's temple, and it seems to be okay with God. There's some Chaos in the garden, yet God calls it good. That's odd, to say the least. (page 27)

Scripture in This Chapter

Genesis 1:21	Ezekiel 44:14
Revelation 12:7	Genesis 2:8
Genesis 2:15	Romans 12:2
Numbers 3:7–8	Philippians 2:5
1 Chronicles 23:32	John 20:14–15

Thoughts, Insights, Questions

_____

_____

_____

_____

_____

I want to remember . . .

_____

_____

_____

Chapter 4

A Dragon in the Garden

That is what we are all wired for. It is the common dream that drives our species. We all want to kill the beasts, slay the dragons, overcome the monsters, and restore peace and order to the temple of creation. We're all standing in front of our own trees of knowledge, facing off with our own beasts and trying our best to defeat them. Which means the original story of Adam and Eve has something to teach us. (page 40)

Scripture in This Chapter

Genesis 3:14

Isaiah 27:1

Amos 9:3

Revelation 12:3, 9

Genesis 3:15

Thoughts, Insights, Questions

_____

_____

_____

_____

_____

I want to remember . . .

_____

_____

_____

After You Read

How does this book's take on the creation account differ from what you remembered? Flip back to your stab at writing about the creation story before you read any of these chapters. Do you look at this story any differently now? What details stand out that you hadn't noticed before?

_____

_____

_____

_____

_____

Look back at your chapter notes, and gather everything you wrote after "I want to remember . . ." here in this space. These are the thoughts and questions you want to bring to your group.

_____

_____

_____

_____

_____

_____

_____

_____

_____

_____

Take a moment now to say a prayer for your group before you gather, asking the Holy Spirit to guide the conversation.

After You Read

A WORLD OF CHAOS: FIRST HALF

All Together

Opening Prayer (5 min.)

Begin your time in prayer, asking God to join you during this time of study.

Overview of Scripture and Content from *Crushing Chaos* (10 min.)

Take turns reading the scriptures referenced below and the related passages from the book. Try to give every person in the group a chance to look up a scripture passage or read the given chapter excerpt.

Genesis 1:1–2, 6–7, 9

I hope we can recover this ancient emphasis. Because the same sovereign Creator who pulled creation out of the Chaos *then* wants to rescue our lives from Chaos *now*. The Bible provides a path from Chaos to Order, and as I began to discover that path for myself and teach it to others, I started seeing less and less anxiety. (From chapter 1: Panic in the Lobby)

1 Corinthians 6:19–20

Our primary function as humans is to reflect the image and likeness of almighty God and to order our lives according to the reality that we are image bearers. That is the predominant reason we were created. It is our central function and our chief end. It is of first importance and occupies the place of primary priority.

We unleash chaos when we

are ignorant of our true function,
rebel against our true function,
attempt to redefine our function.

And we rob ourselves of rest. Because *where* you rest will dictate *how* you rest. (From chapter 2: Peace in the Temple)

Genesis 2:15

The Chaos monsters in the cosmos prove that Adam and Eve have work to do, chaos to tame, order to spread, and adversity to overcome. Their role as image bearers gives them function, but the presence of the *tannin* gives them work and mission. And the talking *tannin* in the garden means they must be wise, alert, and on guard. The Garden of Eden is not a vacation. There's chaos to conquer, a wilderness to subdue. (From chapter 3: Monsters in the Bible)

Revelation 12:9

If temples represent Order, then dragons symbolize Chaos.

Which means Adam and Eve were deceived by a Chaos monster and thus became partners in bringing Chaos into the cosmos. So often we simply conclude that Genesis 3 is the moment that sin entered our world, but I think it may be helpful to introduce some ancient language into our vocabulary. The ancients would've seen Genesis 3 as the moment that the untamable force of Chaos broke into our culture.

This is helpful because it reframes our thinking: Anxiety isn't a sin, but it's a form of chaos. Poverty isn't a sin, but it creates chaos. Suffering and sickness aren't sin. But the reason God tells Job about Leviathan when He finally responds is because suffering can easily produce chaos. (From chapter 4: A Dragon in the Garden)

Our Questions (20–30 min.)

Flip back to the "After You Read" portion of this session. What questions, thoughts, and insights do you have for one another? Was anything confusing or particularly illuminating?

Explore the following questions if you have time. You don't have to go in order—stick with the questions that sound interesting and cover new ground in your discussion.

- What is the actual cure for Chaos? What false cures do we tend to substitute for the real thing?
- What does the seventh day of the creation story teach us about our needs?
- Why does God unravel chaos instead of fixing us instantly?

- Name some of the differences in the ways modern readers and ancient readers interact with the creation story told in Genesis 1.
- In what way does your main goal in life—what you understand to be your chief end—determine whether or not your life is chaotic?
- What realities are present in our lives because we are made in the image of God?
- What does the word *tannin* mean? Which words or phrases are used in our translations for that term? What words or phrases help you understand the term's original intent?
- What are some signs of chaos in the soul?
- How do our modern-day imaginings of the creation story tame it or make it boring? What are the sources of those kinds of perceptions?
- What do the Old Testament texts promise about Christ? What will He be able to do?

In My Life (10 min.)

How have you seen Chaos in your own life?

Try to give each person in the group who wants to share a minute or two to do so.

Closing Prayer (5 min.)

Close in prayer, thanking God for the way He is already working in your minds and hearts.

Make sure to write down the name of each group member so you can pray for them throughout the week.

SESSION 2

A WORLD OF CHAOS: SECOND HALF

On Your Own

Chapter 5: Rolling in the Deep

Chapter 6: Drowning in the Darkness

Chapter 7: Adapting to the Desert

Before You Read

The Chaos described in Genesis has all the power of something truly ancient and all the relevance of something that happens to us every day. Maybe the scope of the creation story is different for you now, and my prayer is that you've felt the awe that these symbols inspire. Gone forever, at least I hope, is the image of a small, unassuming snake wrapped around a tree in a well-manicured garden. We're dealing with *dragons*—we always were.

In this session, we're going to keep unpacking the symbols of Chaos that appear in Genesis and throughout God's Word. But before we do, I want to get a little personal. It's just us here, and you don't need to share any of this with your group. I want you to go back to a chaotic memory and describe below what you can remember. It doesn't have to be the worst thing that ever happened to you. But I want you to focus on a single memory rather than a chain of events. Describe something chaotic that has occurred in your life.

_____

_____

_____

_____

_____

In that moment, what was lacking? The easy answer, of course, is order. But I want you to make a more personal application. How would order have been different?

_____

_____

As you read the next three chapters, we'll work through the specific symbolism in the words used to describe Chaos in the Hebrew text. These ancient, awe-inspiring words are *hosek, tehom, mayim,* and *tohu va-vohu.*

How do they apply to me—or to any person in the twenty-first century? That's what we'll find out as we read. This story doesn't just have wisdom for us—it's about us too.

Before you start reading, spend some time in prayer for yourself and the others in your group.

While You Read

As you read each chapter, use these pages to take notes, make outlines, highlight definitions, or write out what is confusing to you or why you disagree with me. There are no right or wrong answers here.

Keep in mind that reading the content and taking a few notes beforehand is a great way to prepare some thoughts for your study group. Maybe someone else needs to ponder your question or hear your insight—you're not just doing this for yourself.

So, while you read each chapter, I want you to use this study guide to do these three things:

1. Note any scripture passages that stand out to you.
2. Write out thoughts or copy phrases that connect dots for you or spark wonder, confusion, anger, or disagreement.
3. Summarize your experience, questions, or insights about the chapter in the "I want to remember . . ." section—the one thing you want to bring up to your group.

Chapter 5

Rolling in the Deep

It's the same one we've all heard—the voice that deceives us into believing we can handle the pressure of the chaos that inevitably accompanies our sin or circumstances. (page 48)

Scripture in This Chapter

Genesis 1:2   Genesis 2:24
Revelation 21:1   Matthew 5:37
Genesis 1:4

Thoughts, Insights, Questions

_____
_____
_____
_____
_____

I want to remember . . .

_____
_____
_____

Chapter 6

Drowning in the Darkness

It's not shocking to me that the Bible equates
darkness with chaos and that the chaos of
Genesis 1:2 isn't fully encapsulated by the sea or
the raging flood; it also includes the darkness of
the wilderness. (page 60)

Scripture in This Chapter

Genesis 1:2–3   John 1:4

John 1:3–5   Proverbs 29:18

John 8:12   Ephesians 4:18

Revelation 21:23–25   Romans 1:21–22

Thoughts, Insights, Questions

_____

_____

_____

_____

_____

I want to remember . . .

_____

_____

_____

Chapter 7

Adapting to the Desert

The Dragon has convinced most of us that the desert wilderness we're living in is really a garden. There are trees. There's fruit. There are rivers. Garden spaces and wilderness spaces share so much in common. So, we compromise and settle—out in the wilderness—and we lie to and convince ourselves that the desert is a suitable home for our souls. (pages 65–66)

Scripture in This Chapter

Genesis 1:2   Jeremiah 4:23
Isaiah 34:11

Thoughts, Insights, Questions

_____

_____

_____

_____

_____

I want to remember . . .

_____

_____

_____

After You Read

The desert—harsh, barren, wild. The darkness—complete and overpowering.

The deep—unknown, unforgiving; the home of monsters.

Which of these symbols resonates most with the chaos you described before you read these chapters? Why?

_____

_____

_____

_____

_____

Look back at your chapter notes, and gather everything you wrote after "I want to remember . . ." here in this space. These are the thoughts and questions you want to bring to your group.

_____

_____

_____

_____

_____

_____

_____

_____

_____

_____

_____

_____

_____

_____

_____

Take a moment now to say a prayer for your group before you gather, asking the Holy Spirit to guide the conversation. Flip back to the space where you wrote every person's name so you can pray for them personally.

A WORLD OF CHAOS: SECOND HALF

All Together

Opening Prayer (5 min.)

Begin your time in prayer, asking God to join you during this time of study.

Overview of Scripture and Content from *Crushing Chaos* (10 min.)

Take turns reading the scriptures referenced below and the related passages from the book. Try to give every person in the group a chance to look up a scripture passage or read the given chapter excerpt.

Matthew 5:37

Whether you're drowning in the chaos of people pleasing or in the chaos of sin, God's grace will pull you out of the depths of the *tehom* and rescue you from the undertow of the raging floodwaters. Moreover, no matter what kind of chaos you're drowning in, you need to establish healthier and stronger boundaries in your life. Because people pleasing is the result of not establishing good boundaries with others and sin is the result of not establishing good boundaries with yourself. (From chapter 5: Rolling in the Deep)

John 1:3–5

Simply put, when there's *darkness,* there's no *discipline.* And when there's no discipline, there's darkness.

Maybe you've diagnosed yourself as someone who doesn't have much discipline. Keep in mind that discipline is the result of a life that is full of vision and foresight. I promise you, it's a whole lot easier to practice discipline *today* when you're living for *tomorrow.* (From chapter 6: Drowning in the Darkness)

Hebrews 3:16–19

When Yahweh finally commanded them to leave the desert behind and invade the land of Canaan, they refused. Because the chaos of the desert has a gravitational pull. It doesn't let us go easily.

The biblical authors describe the land of Canaan using garden imagery and symbols. It was lush, fertile, and fruitful—a new Eden of sorts. A garden for God's people who were stuck wandering in the wilderness. But a garden is a difficult space to occupy if you've become comfortable in the desert. (From chapter 7: Adapting to the Desert)

Our Questions (20–30 min.)

Flip back to the "After You Read" portion of this session. What questions, thoughts, and insights do you have for one another? Was anything confusing or particularly illuminating?

Explore the following questions if you have time. You don't have to go in order—stick with the questions that sound interesting and cover new ground in your discussion.

- How do you understand the word *boundaries*? Has the concept of boundaries been helpful to you? Do you think it ever gets misused? If so, what does that look like?
- Describe the link between order and boundaries.
- Review the four symbols of Chaos in Genesis 1:2, linking each with its Hebrew term.
- What kinds of things flourish in darkness, and how does darkness help them flourish?
- The elements of divine Order are sequence, hierarchy, rhythm, function, separation, and boundaries. Which of these have resonated with you as you've read? Have any been challenging to you?
- How does a person become comfortable in Chaos? What does that kind of life look like?
- The Hebrew word for "desert" is *tohu va-vohu*. If you read this term as "wilderness" rather than "formless," how would that shift your understanding of the contrast between the *tohu va-vohu* and the Garden of Eden?
- This first part of the book has been about discovering the symbols used for Order and Chaos in the Bible, drawing on the story of creation, the history of the Israelites, and the book of Revelation. Pair the symbols for Order and Chaos—for exam-

ple, light and darkness. Which of these images appeals the most to your imagination, and why?

In My Life (10 min.)

Have you ever felt comfortable in Chaos? You don't have to give the details. Does the description of the deep, the dark, and/or the desert fit your experience?

Try to give each person in the group who wants to share a minute or two to do so.

Closing Prayer (5 min.)

Close in prayer, thanking God for the infinite ways He orders the world.

Last week, you wrote down group members' names to pray for them throughout the week. This week, you can do the same thing, especially if you've had someone else join you.

_____

_____

_____

_____

_____

Also, just a warning before you go: You'll read more chapters for sessions 3 and 4 than you have yet, so plan accordingly. The format of the study stays the same; you'll just be reading more. For sessions 5 and 6, we'll slow down again as we take a deep dive into how Jesus Christ deals with Chaos.

SESSION 3

TAMING THE BEAST

On Your Own

Before You Read

The mighty waters. The wild desert. The gigantic, awe-inspiring monsters, swimming in the depths. The encompassing dark. Genesis has a setting that is truly cosmic in scope. Yet there's something in Genesis we haven't talked about very much yet: the beasts. Not the monsters but the beasts.

When I started studying Genesis, I realized that the stories at the beginning of the Bible were both stranger and more relevant to my life than anything I could have imagined. I had passed over the words before, sure—but I hadn't heard them yet. I want you to read these chapters with your Bible open, right at those Genesis pages, because there will be things you've never noticed before. You're going to want to double-check, thinking, *Does it really say that?* At least that's what I did the whole time I was diving into the text. Those chapters took on totally new dimensions for me, and I hope they do for you too.

But before we get there, I have an important question for you: How are humans and animals different? This can be more of a chart than an essay.

We've heard a lot about what Genesis says concerning the world we live in. In these next chapters, we'll read together what Genesis says about people—the creation most beloved of God. The creation everything else was created for.

Before you start reading, spend some time in prayer for yourself and the others in your group.

While You Read

As you read each chapter, use these pages to take notes, make outlines, highlight definitions, or write out what is confusing to you or why you disagree with me. There are no right or wrong answers here.

Keep in mind that reading the content and taking a few notes beforehand is a great way to prepare some thoughts for your study group. Maybe someone else needs to ponder your question or hear your insight—you're not just doing this for yourself.

So, while you read each chapter, I want you to use this study guide to do these three things:

1. Note any scripture passages that stand out to you. We're going to cover an incredible amount of scripture in this section. Please don't feel like you need to do an intensive study on each verse.

2. Write out thoughts or copy phrases that connect dots for you or spark wonder, confusion, anger, or disagreement. There's a spot to include the names of the Genesis characters you read about, from Adam to Joseph. This is optional. Use it if it helps you keep track.

3. Summarize your experience, questions, or insights about the chapter in the "I want to remember . . ." section—the one thing you want to bring up to your group.

Chapter 8

You Son of a Beast

What does it mean to be truly human?

When we find the answer to that question, we find the key to establishing Order and conquering Chaos. By recovering our humanity, we recover Order. But by continuing to live as beasts, we multiply Chaos. So, let's dive further into Genesis and find out how to be truly human by slaying the beasts living within us and taming the Chaos that surrounds us. (page 78)

Scripture in This Chapter

Genesis 4:7

Genesis 3:15

Genesis 2:19–20

Genesis 3:1, 14

Genesis 4:8

Genesis 1:26

Genesis Characters

_____

_____

Thoughts, Insights, Questions

_____

_____

_____

_____

_____

I want to remember . . .

_____

_____

_____

Chapter 9

Hagar and Her Wild Ass

The lying, murdering Chaos Dragon from Genesis has certainly fathered offspring, and we're going to continue to track the genealogy of those children so we can retain and restore our humanity and thus establish Order. (page 84)

Scripture in This Chapter

John 8:44

Genesis 16:12

Genesis 22:1–3, 7–8

Genesis 25:25, 27

Genesis 27:15–16

Genesis 25:26

Genesis 3:15

Genesis Characters

_____

_____

_____

Thoughts, Insights, Questions

_____

_____

_____

_____

_____

I want to remember . . .

_____

_____

_____

Chapter 10

A Ladder in Luz

> He's done absolutely nothing to deserve a divine
> visitation. Yet that's exactly what happens,
> because the grace of God often shows up when
> we least expect it and least deserve it. (page 91)

Scripture in This Chapter

Isaiah 61:6

Exodus 19:3, 5–6

1 Peter 2:9

Genesis 28:11–15

Exodus 19:6

John 1:51

Genesis 11:4

Genesis 11:3

Genesis 6:14

Acts 8:1

Acts 1:8–9

Genesis Characters

_____

_____

Thoughts, Insights, Questions

_____

_____

_____

_____

_____

I want to remember . . .

_____

_____

_____

Chapter 11

Limping with Laban

These stories are intentional parallels. And Laban
has replaced Jacob as the new snake. For the
first time in his life, Jacob can empathize with his
brother, Esau, and finally understand the pain of
being deceived by a trusted family member.
Jacob, like Esau, has now experienced
irreparable and irreversible betrayal. (page 100)

Scripture in This Chapter

Genesis 29:20–21   Genesis 32:1, 24–25, 31

Genesis Characters

_____

_____

Thoughts, Insights, Questions

_____

_____

_____

_____

I want to remember . . .

_____

_____

_____

Chapter 12

Caged but Not a Beast

A fierce animal has devoured Joseph. A wild animal. A beast of the field. A monster of Chaos.

We know that Joseph wasn't actually devoured, so technically their father is incorrect. But we also know that since the Bible speaks in the language of looping symbols and repeating images, Jacob is actually spot on. Joseph has been devoured by fierce and wild animals—his brothers. Which reveals that his brothers are the offspring of the Serpent. (pages 106–107)

Scripture in This Chapter

Ephesians 6:12

Genesis 37:31–33

Genesis 37:26–28

Genesis 39:6–9, 19–20

Genesis 40:1–3, 20–22

Genesis 37:23

Genesis 39:12

Genesis 37:8, 33–34

Genesis 45:3–4

Genesis 42:6

Genesis 4:7

Genesis 50:20

John 10:17–18

Genesis Characters

Thoughts, Insights, Questions

_____

_____

_____

_____

_____

I want to remember . . .

_____

_____

_____

Chapter 13

Pierced Ears and Empty Stomachs

Scripture is teaching us, in a very subtle and
Eastern way, that humans and beasts are not
designed to be partners. Adam is designed to
rule over them, not partner with them. Adam
belongs in the garden. The beasts of the field
belong in the wild. God and Adam therefore reject
all beasts as suitable partners for humanity.
Humans are humans; beasts are beasts. They are
categorically different in every way, and Adam
has been set apart from the beasts of the field.
(page 114)

Scripture in This Chapter

Philippians 3:18–19

Genesis 2:18–20

Genesis 3:1

2 Corinthians 2:11

Exodus 21:5–6

Philippians 1:21

1 Corinthians 9:19

Genesis Characters

_____

_____

Thoughts, Insights, Questions

_____

_____

_____

_____

_____

I want to remember . . .

_____

_____

_____

After You Read

Which Genesis character caught you as you read through these stories? Maybe it's a person you related to in a new way or someone whom your perspective changed about—*I didn't understand that they felt pain like that.* In your own words, describe the story of one of the Genesis characters.

_____

_____

_____

_____

_____

Look back at your chapter notes, and gather everything you wrote after "I want to remember . . ." here in this space. These are the thoughts and questions you want to bring to your group.

_____

_____

_____

_____

_____

_____

_____

_____

_____

_____

_____

_____

_____

Take a moment now to say a prayer for your group before you gather, asking the Holy Spirit to guide the conversation. Flip back to the space where you wrote every person's name so you can pray for them personally.

SESSION 3

TAMING THE BEAST

All Together

Opening Prayer (5 min.)

Begin your time in prayer, asking God to join you during this time of study.

Overview of Scripture and Content from *Crushing Chaos* (10 min.)

Take turns reading the scriptures referenced below and the related passages from the book. Try to give every person in the group a chance to look up a scripture passage or read the given chapter excerpt.

Genesis 4:7–8

Genesis teaches us that it is very easy for humans to slip into beast mode and begin to exhibit animal-like behavior. You allow the beast to take you into the field and rob you of your humanity

every time your temper gets the best of you,
every time your lusts and your passions rule you,
every time your instincts overtake your intentions,
every time your primal urges aren't conquered,
every time gossip and negativity erupt from your heart and
flow from your lips.
(From chapter 8: You Son of a Beast)

John 8:44

Sometimes the Bible shows us how humans lose their humanity and chronicles their descent into animal-like tendencies. But then sometimes it shows us that God can take a heel-grabbing, deceptive, and crafty beast of a man like Jacob and restore his humanity through an epic journey. Which gives me a whole lot of hope because I, too, have failed to tame the beast and conquer the chaos. So have you. But we're not beyond redemption. God is in the business of not only ordering our world but also ordering us. He is in the business of taking broken humans like us and making us whole. (From chapter 9: Hagar and Her Wild Ass)

Genesis 28:11–12

Would Jacob build another tower, or would he build a temple?
Will we build towers of Babel or temples of the Holy Spirit?
Will we build bridges for God or attempt to build towers to
reach God?

Each represents a very different way of being human.
Jacob sees a vision of the kind of human God has called him to

be. He leaves Luz knowing that he is called to be not a heel grabber but a ladder that Yahweh can use to deliver grace and shalom to humanity. (From chapter 10: A Ladder in Luz)

Genesis 32:24–25

So, Jacob must limp back home to meet Esau. God doesn't allow him to show up in strength but causes him to return limping. Jacob has to trust that God will protect him and that maybe his brother is no longer a beast. (From chapter 11: Limping with Laban)

Philippians 1:12–14

This is the secret to preserving our humanity—by retaining our power and authority. The Dragon's agenda is to divide and conquer, so I'm playing right into his hands when I villainize and demonize those who have hurt me. The reason I forgave my father is that I was tired of him having more power over me than I had over myself. I was tired of the Beast using my father to control me. (From chapter 12: Caged but Not a Beast)

Exodus 21:5–6

This is an invitation to dethrone the god of self. To give your life away in service and love to the people of God. This is your opportunity to leave independence and selfishness behind—to reject rampant individualism, to lose your life so you can find it. It's your invitation to be truly human. To step into the metaphorical doorway and allow the Master of the universe to pierce your ear and mark you as His and His alone, and to hear His voice through your ears and yours alone. (From chapter 13: Pierced Ears and Empty Stomachs)

Our Questions (20–30 min.)

Flip back to the "After You Read" portion of this session. What questions, thoughts, and insights do you have for one another? Was anything confusing or particularly illuminating?

Explore the following questions if you have time. You don't have to go in order—stick with the questions that sound interesting and cover new ground in your discussion.

- What signals in Scripture tell the reader that something is significant? Are these kinds of patterns naturally obvious to you, or is it challenging to find them?
- Which faults have you heard chalked up to "being human"?
- How do we see the human-beast pairing play out through the Genesis stories?
- What is the function of the "great High Priest"? What is He able to do for us?
- What capacities do we gain when we experience pain, loss, and suffering?
- Describe a Genesis parallel that surprised you.
- In your own words, based on your reflections of the reading and scripture, summarize the message of Genesis.
- As Manny describes them, what three changing perspectives of their parents do young people undergo (see chapter 12)? Do you think these are accurate?
- What do we do when we villainize others? How does it affect us?

- What distinction does Rabbi David Fohrman (in chapter 13) make about the way God speaks to animals versus the way He speaks to humans? What does this say about the differences in the natures of humans and beasts?
- Why do we give so much credence to our feelings, urges, and instincts? Is there a way to acknowledge them without making them more significant than they are?
- How does God turn monsters back into men and women? Use a Genesis example.

In My Life (10 min.)

Which Genesis character resonated with you the most? Who helped you see someone like yourself in these ancient stories?

Try to give each person in the group who wants to share a minute or two to do so.

Closing Prayer (5 min.)

Close in prayer, thanking God that through His power we can actually change.

Make a note to pray for everyone in your group by name (including anyone who couldn't make it today), especially if you've had someone else join you.

_____

_____

_____

_____

_____

SESSION 4

COME HELL OR HIGH WATER

On Your Own

Before You Read

The words of Genesis are an invitation to God's Order. But maybe you have some hesitations with this, and I wouldn't blame you. Maybe you've been in Christian spheres long enough to hear the phrase "Old Testament God." You know, the *mean* God. And Jesus is the nice one. Even with all the nuance in the world, this is the wrong idea. I know how the sermons and studies went: God destroyed. God raged. God killed. All because of what humans did—humans *like you*. How are you supposed to think that He won't do the same thing with you?

But I want to introduce you to a different Old Testament God. One who is trustworthy and full of *grace*. We don't have to wait for the smaller half of the Bible to see His grace.

Let's start this round with the Flood narrative. Give me your version of this story in Genesis. It starts with a guy named Noah. What happened to him? More importantly, *why* did God do what He did next? Don't open your Bible yet. I'm interested in what you remember.

_____

_____

_____

_____

_____

The next chapters are all about water. And as we'll discover together, this water is a water of renewal. Reordering. What God unleashes is a flood of grace.

Before you start reading, spend some time in prayer for yourself and the others in your group.

While You Read

As you read each chapter, use these pages to take notes, make outlines, highlight definitions, or write out what is confusing to you or why you disagree with me. There are no right or wrong answers here.

Keep in mind that reading the content and taking a few notes beforehand is a great way to prepare some thoughts for your study group. Maybe someone else needs to ponder your question or hear your insight—you're not just doing this for yourself.

So, while you read each chapter, I want you to use this study guide to do these three things:

1. Note any scripture passages that stand out to you. We're going to cover an incredible amount of scripture in this section. Please don't feel like you need to do an intensive study on each verse.
2. Write out thoughts or copy phrases that connect dots for you or spark wonder, confusion, anger, or disagreement.
3. Summarize your experience, questions, or insights about the chapter in the "I want to remember . . ." section—the one thing you want to bring up to your group.

Chapter 14

When God Leaves the Group Chat

The Flood account isn't a story of God destroying the earth. Rather it is a story of how we turned our ordered home into a hell of Chaos, and it only took seven chapters of the biblical story for us to do it. Humans desired a world without God, and when God removed Himself, creation simply reverted to its original state—chaos. (page 126)

Scripture in This Chapter

Genesis 7:11   Romans 1:24
Revelation 21:1   1 Samuel 16:14

Thoughts, Insights, Questions

I want to remember . . .

Chapter 15

The Context of Chaos

The story of the Flood in Scripture can easily be taken out of context. It's not hard to conclude that God is unfair and unjustly vengeful. But before we jump to that conclusion and create chaos, let's actually place the *content* of Genesis into *context*. (page 133)

Scripture in This Chapter

Genesis 6:3

Genesis 11:10–32

Genesis 7:11

Genesis 6:11–13

Psalm 93:1

Thoughts, Insights, Questions

_____

_____

_____

_____

_____

I want to remember . . .

_____

_____

_____

Chapter 16

Noah's Temple

God brings order to chaos by creating temple spaces. Out of the chaos of creation, God planted a temple garden. And out of the chaos of the Flood, God had Noah construct a floating temple that sustained human life amid the chaotic floodwaters. However, the Bible doesn't *tell* us that Noah's ark was a temple. It *shows* us. (pages 144–145)

Scripture in This Chapter

Genesis 6:14–16   Hebrews 9:2–4
1 Kings 6:2   Genesis 8:20
John 10:9   Genesis 6:22
Genesis 6:21   Exodus 40:16
Exodus 16:32–33   Psalm 46:1–3

Thoughts, Insights, Questions

_____

_____

_____

_____

_____

I want to remember . . .

_____

_____

_____

Chapter 17

Passive Wrath and Active Grace

When God departs from His creation or removes Himself from our lives, everything inevitably folds in on itself and sinks back into Chaos. That's how the passive wrath of God works. But we must acknowledge the flip side of the coin—active grace. (pages 152–153)

Scripture in This Chapter

Genesis 2:17   Genesis 9:12–16

Psalm 51:11   John 19:34

2 Samuel 6:21–22

Thoughts, Insights, Questions

_____

_____

_____

_____

_____

I want to remember . . .

_____

_____

_____

Chapter 18

Moses and His Dragon

All of these are popular examples of the Mandela effect. However, this phenomenon extends beyond pop culture. For myriad reasons, many Christians have communal false memories of biblical stories and events. (page 160)

Scripture in This Chapter

Exodus 7:10

Exodus 2:10

Exodus 1:10–14

Genesis 10:8–12

Ezekiel 29:2–3

Exodus 14:28–29

Isaiah 51:9–10

Thoughts, Insights, Questions

_____

_____

_____

_____

_____

I want to remember . . .

_____

_____

_____

Chapter 19

Plagues of Chaos

It could easily seem as though Yahweh is being unjust, extreme, and unreasonably cruel as the plagues pull Egypt back into Chaos. But we must unearth the context beneath the surface before we jump to conclusions. The Flood narrative has already established that Yahweh is loving, gracious, kind, and merciful, and this account of the plagues cannot erase or undermine that. (page 166)

Scripture in This Chapter

Genesis 1:9–10

Exodus 7:19–20

Genesis 1:11

Exodus 12:12

Numbers 33:3–4

1 Corinthians 10:20–21

John 14:15

Thoughts, Insights, Questions

_____

_____

_____

_____

_____

I want to remember . . .

_____

_____

_____

Chapter 20

A Portal Back to Eden

Can you think of another time when the
construction of something was split into a seven-
part process? Yeah, the creation account in
Genesis. (page 175)

Scripture in This Chapter

Exodus 25–30   Genesis 1:28, 31

Exodus 31:1–17   Exodus 40:33

Proverbs 8:22–24   Genesis 2:1–2

Exodus 39:43   Genesis 3:24

Thoughts, Insights, Questions

_____

_____

_____

_____

_____

I want to remember . . .

_____

_____

_____

After You Read

We've been looking through the scriptures at the history of God's people from creation, to the Flood, to the establishment of the nation of Israel, to their slavery and ransom. As inconstant and changing as the people can be, God remains the same—faithful, all-powerful, and trustworthy.

I want you to make a brief history of your own life, breaking it up into phases if you like. How has your perspective of God changed over time, through your own history?

_____

_____

_____

_____

_____

I've tried to make the argument through these last chapters that God's character hasn't changed. He is gracious and merciful, willing to make the greatest sacrifices Himself. Take a moment to respond to the following statement however you need to: God is trustworthy.

_____

_____

Look back at your chapter notes, and gather everything you wrote after "I want to remember . . ." here in this space. These are the thoughts and questions you want to bring to your group.

_____

_____

_____

_____

_____

_____

_____

_____

_____

_____

_____

_____

_____

_____

Take a moment now to say a prayer for your group before you gather, asking the Holy Spirit to guide the conversation. Flip back to the space where you wrote every person's name so you can pray for them personally.

COME HELL
OR HIGH WATER

All Together

Opening Prayer (5 min.)

Begin your time in prayer, asking God to join you during this time of study.

Overview of Scripture and Content from *Crushing Chaos* (10 min.)

Take turns reading the scriptures referenced below and the related passages from the book. Try to give every person in the group a chance to look up a scripture passage or read the given chapter excerpt.

Revelation 21:1

It's impossible to trust God's Order if we can't trust His character. God doesn't drown people; Chaos does. And we have partnered with Chaos to our own detriment and downfall. All God has to do to punish us is simply get up and walk away. That's it. When God leaves, everything is inevitably plunged back into Chaos. (From chapter 14: When God Leaves the Group Chat)

Genesis 6:13

Whether you're stuck in the chaos of literalism or the chaos of secularism and deconstruction, the invitation is the same. I'm inviting you to behold the beauty of the Scriptures based on their cultural, historical, and linguistic context and discover for yourself what God has *said*—and, more importantly, what He *means* by what He's said. (From chapter 15: The Context of Chaos)

Psalm 46:1–3

Maybe the ark is more than a boat. Perhaps it is a dwelling place for God. It could be that the world needed ordered sacred space so we could dwell with God again.

Maybe you feel like God is offering you a temple when your circumstances suggest you need a boat. Maybe you need to restore order to your chaotic life and don't see how a temple is relevant to your problems. Allow me to help. God's Order precedes His presence, and His presence always leads us into more order. (From chapter 16: Noah's Temple)

John 19:34

Yahweh is saying to Noah and to all humanity, "Next time I flood the earth with water, it will be because the arrow pierced Me, not y'all." The proof that humanity and Yahweh are in covenant is the fact that He's willing to be on the receiving end of the archer's arrow rather than make us pay the penalty of our sin. His covenant with Noah is essentially Yahweh saying, "This is going to hurt Me more than it's going to hurt you"—and actually meaning it. (From chapter 17: Passive Wrath and Active Grace)

Exodus 1:11–14

Pharaoh has unleashed a level of chaos that we have yet to see in the biblical narrative. The writer of Exodus links him to the patterns of Chaos we've already seen, while highlighting that something unprecedented is also happening in the story. We've never seen an international superpower enslave an entire ethnic group, countless baby boys drowned in the Nile by a tyrant, or a world leader who claims to be the incarnation of a god.

We've seen Chaos, but not like this. (From chapter 18: Moses and His Dragon)

Numbers 33:3–4

Yahweh always liberates His people not only from the sin of slavery but also from the slavery of sin—both then and now. (From chapter 19: Plagues of Chaos)

Exodus 25:8–9

The construction of the tabernacle isn't about building. It's about new creation, and the same Creator who pulled this world out of Chaos is at work again with a new fledgling nation of freed slaves. The construction of the tabernacle is about Order ruling over Chaos—Sabbath rest and reentry into Eden and God providing refuge for His people amid chaotic waters and ravenous wilderness. (From chapter 20: A Portal Back to Eden)

Our Questions (20–30 min.)

Flip back to the "After You Read" portion of this session. What questions, thoughts, and insights do you have for one another? Was anything confusing or particularly illuminating?

Explore the following questions if you have time. You don't have to go in order—stick with the questions that sound interesting and cover new ground in your discussion.

- Did your perspective on the story of Noah and the Flood change because of these chapters? If so, in what way?
- We exist in the context of our own time, thousands of years after Scripture was written. What tools and attitudes do we need to approach Scripture with to grasp its meaning?
- According to Manny, what's the significance of the 120 years referred to in Genesis 6:3?
- What do we know about the original audience of Genesis? How does becoming more familiar with the context of the audience help us understand Scripture, particularly these first books or the Gospels?
- In your own words, explain the difference between God's passive and active wrath.
- What implications and foreshadowing do we find in the Flood narrative if we understand the "bow" in Genesis 9 to be an archer's bow?
- Many signals—repeated images—throughout Exodus link the story of the Israelites to the stories in Genesis. Name a few of these links.

- The books of prophecy in the Old Testament reveal Pharaoh's character. What symbol do the prophets compare Pharaoh to?
- How do the plagues reveal the effects of God's passive wrath? Think of the ways that the plagues are reversals of God's ordering work in creation.
- What's the difference between monotheism and a monolatrous worldview? (Look in chapter 19.)
- By leading His people out of Egypt, God was restoring order to them. How do you think the Israelites would have been affected by generations of slavery? What kinds of practices and beliefs about themselves would they have picked up?
- Has your view on the purpose of Scripture—and the most helpful ways to read it—changed over the last few weeks?

In My Life (10 min.)

Is God trustworthy? What beliefs, experiences, or challenges do you bring to that question?

Try to give each person in the group who wants to share a minute or two to do so.

Closing Prayer (5 min.)

Close in prayer, thanking God for leading us into freedom. Make a note to pray for everyone in your group by name (including anyone who couldn't make it today), especially if you've had someone else join you.

THE PRINCE OF PEACE: FIRST HALF

On Your Own

Before You Read

Maybe you've already been connecting how the signs and symbols we see in Genesis and the other books of the Old Testament relate to the ultimate Crusher of chaos—the Prince of Peace, Jesus Christ. Don't worry if things aren't falling into place. It's all right to stand in the middle of the mystery. Paradox—the simultaneous existence of contradictory things—may be uncomfortable for us, but the writers of the original texts lived and breathed it. At this point in our study, I hope the Scriptures have become more mysterious to you, not less.

Chaos. *Tehom. Tovu va-vohu.* Ancient words that all appear in the stories of Jesus we read in the Gospels. Now we're going to find out how they are relevant in His story. Turns out, He knows Genesis pretty well. Almost like He was there, right?

But before we begin, I'd like to hear from you. Who is Jesus Christ? And why does He still matter?

_____

_____

_____

_____

_____

In the final section of the book and the next two sessions of study, we turn our attention to Jesus and the span of years He walked on earth, revealing Himself as the Chaos-crushing God of the Jewish scriptures.

Before you start reading, spend some time in prayer for yourself and the others in your group.

While You Read

As you read each chapter, use these pages to take notes, make outlines, highlight definitions, or write out what is confusing to you or why you disagree with me. There are no right or wrong answers here.

Keep in mind that reading the content and taking a few notes beforehand is a great way to prepare some thoughts for your study group. Maybe someone else needs to ponder your question or hear your insight—you're not just doing this for yourself.

So, while you read each chapter, I want you to use this study guide to do these three things:

1. Note any scripture passages that stand out to you.
2. Write out thoughts or copy phrases that connect dots for you or spark wonder, confusion, anger, or disagreement.
3. Summarize your experience, questions, or insights about the chapter in the "I want to remember . . ." section—the one thing you want to bring up to your group.

Chapter 21

Breaking the Cycle of Chaos

So far, then, we have Chaos, water, wind, word, and Order. We're five steps into our six-step pattern, and the pattern will always end with a test. (page 182)

Scripture in This Chapter

Genesis 6:5   Joshua 4:1

Genesis 8:8, 15–16   Joshua 7:1

Exodus 14:21   Joshua 13:1–2

Numbers 14:22–23   Judges 2:7–11

Joshua 3:15–17   Matthew 3:13–17

Thoughts, Insights, Questions

_____

_____

_____

_____

_____

I want to remember . . .

_____

_____

_____

Chapter 22

Plunder the Dragon

Not only does Jesus go out into the desert to demonstrate His authority over His flesh and to tame the wild animals according to the pattern set by Adam, Noah, and Daniel. Jesus also enters the wilderness to confront the Dragon. (page 199)

Scripture in This Chapter

Daniel 4:33	Genesis 3:15
Daniel 6:22–23	Mark 3:27
Daniel 1:8	Genesis 3:24
Genesis 2:20	2 Corinthians 5:21
Genesis 7:7–9	Mark 1:25–26
Mark 1:12–13	

Thoughts, Insights, Questions

_____

_____

_____

_____

_____

I want to remember . . .

_____

_____

_____

Chapter 23

The Tempter and the Tempest

There's a cheat code here, so let's wander into
the wilderness of Jesus's temptation so we can
march out of our personal chaos and confusion.
(page 204)

Scripture in This Chapter

Matthew 4:1–11   1 Corinthians 9:9

Luke 4:13   Luke 8:24

Matthew 16:23   Matthew 8:26

Mark 4:39   Luke 8:22, 25

1 Timothy 5:18

Thoughts, Insights, Questions

_____

_____

_____

_____

_____

I want to remember . . .

_____

_____

_____

One Small Step for Man

We're oddly interconnected and interdependent. . . . Which explains how Peter can conquer the Chaos and walk on the Sea of Galilee, as Matthew's gospel details. Peter sees Jesus do it and therefore knows it is possible. (page 218)

Scripture in This Chapter

Matthew 14:25–29	Job 9:8–9, 11
Mark 6:48	Matthew 14:30–33

Thoughts, Insights, Questions

_____

_____

_____

_____

_____

I want to remember . . .

_____

_____

_____

After You Read

Were you expecting the link between Jesus and Genesis to be so distinct? Once you see it, you can't unsee it. I want you to flip back to the "Before You Read" piece of this session. After these chapters, would you amend or add anything to your description of who Christ is and why He matters?

_____

_____

_____

_____

_____

Write a prayer to the One who, when tested, never failed.

_____

_____

Look back at your chapter notes, and gather everything you wrote after "I want to remember . . ." here in this space. These are the thoughts and questions you want to bring to your group.

_____

_____

_____

_____

_____

_____

_____

_____

_____

_____

_____

_____

_____

Take a moment now to say a prayer for your group before you gather, asking the Holy Spirit to guide the conversation. Flip back to the space where you wrote every person's name so you can pray for them personally.

THE PRINCE OF PEACE: FIRST HALF

All Together

Opening Prayer (5 min.)

Begin your time in prayer, asking God to join you during this time of study.

Overview of Scripture and Content from *Crushing Chaos* (10 min.)

Take turns reading from the scriptures referenced below and the related passages from the book. Try to give every person in the group a chance to look up a scripture passage or read the given chapter excerpt.

Matthew 3:13–17

As we turn to other moments in Jesus's life and ministry, let us remember that His entire ministry started by standing in the floodwaters of the Jordan as an agent of God's Order and a Prince of Peace. Everything Jesus does afterward is colored by the inaugural moment of His baptism and His subsequent wilderness testing. Jesus is the Chaos Crusher. Jesus is the Beast-taming, Dragon-conquering, Chaos-crushing Messiah. Born as the offspring of the woman to crush the head of the Dragon. Born to break the cycle of Chaos so that all God's children may be free. (From chapter 21: Breaking the Cycle of Chaos)

Mark 1:12–13

Adam and Eve are expelled out of the garden.
Jesus is expelled into the wilderness.

Adam and Eve eat the fruit in the garden.
So, Jesus fasts in the wilderness.

Adam and Eve fail to subdue the animal within the garden.
So, Jesus has to subdue the animal within and without in the wilderness.

Jesus was driven out so that we could be brought back in. The wilderness is not our fate. We're not stuck out in the desert. We can return to the garden—we can enter and find rest for our souls. (From chapter 22: Plunder the Dragon)

Luke 8:22–25

Where is their faith? It's obvious, actually. Examine their words: "Master, Master, we're going to drown!" (verse 24). They believe in the power of the storm more than they believe in Jesus.

Their faith is in the storm. Their faith is in the new, rebranded Baal, the storm god.

Because the storm can never get your worship without first getting your faith. And the storm can't get your faith without getting your attention and your focus. (From chapter 23: The Tempter and the Tempest)

Matthew 14:25–33

That's where so many of us are. Life has happened, you've encountered a storm, and the tempest and the Tempter have your ear. You are standing next to Jesus as He's telling you to walk with Him back to the boat, and you are paralyzed.

You've overcome the chaos of fear once before, but now the chaos of trauma has you stuck.

I know exactly how you feel. And so does Peter. (From chapter 24: One Small Step for Man)

Our Questions (20–30 min.)

Flip back to the "After You Read" portion of this session. What questions, thoughts, and insights do you have for one another? Was anything confusing or particularly illuminating?

Explore the following questions if you have time. You don't have to go in order—stick with the questions that sound interesting and cover new ground in your discussion.

- Name the six steps in the Chaos cycle. How is knowing a pattern like this helpful to us as we approach these ancient texts?
- What would the ancient readers of Matthew's gospel have seen as the sixth step in the Chaos cycle? How was Jesus different

from Adam and Eve, the nation of Israel, and the other leaders who came before Him?

- Do you read Jesus's words to His disciples in Mark 3:27 differently now? If so, how?
- Think through the beginning of Jesus's ministry, equipped with any new perspective you gained from these chapters. What hadn't you seen before?
- What three observations did Manny make about the Tempter from Matthew 4:1–11, and do any of them resonate with you? His remarks are at the beginning of chapter 23: The Tempter and the Tempest.
- Which is more difficult: coming up with a plan for order or maintaining that plan? What does this tell us about ourselves?
- How is Satan like Goliath—what weapon were they both relying on? Are the enemies we face often wielding the same thing?
- What is the link between the storm on the Sea of Galilee and Jesus's temptation in the desert?
- How can we muzzle the voice of the Tempter? What has worked for you before?
- What kinds of revelations of Jesus's humanity help you understand Him as both fully God and fully man?
- What does Peter's experience walking on the water teach us about failure?

In My Life (10 min.)

Who is Jesus Christ, and how has He dealt with the chaos in your life?

Try to give each person in the group who wants to share a minute or two to do so.

Closing Prayer (5 min.)

Close in prayer, thanking God for sending Christ into the world to save us. Make a note to pray for everyone in your group by name (including anyone who couldn't make it today), especially if you've had someone else join you.

SESSION 6

THE PRINCE OF PEACE: SECOND HALF

On Your Own

Before You Read

We've established that Jesus came to crush Chaos, wielding all the power of the God who separated the light and dark, the sky and sea. His divine words precede a remarkable reordering—we see miracle after miracle. He even has power over death. But He died anyway.

What explanations and justifications have you heard for this before? Is there anything unsatisfying about them? This is a space for you to consider the plot holes. Or maybe over years of walking in faith, the question about Jesus's death has become a little worn-out for you. Then this is a space for you to describe that.

I want you to consider this and respond to it: The Gospels describe the death of *God*.

_____

_____

_____

_____

_____

This final part of the book will bring Genesis context to the crucifixion and resurrection of Christ, relying on John, the beloved disciple, to carry us to the finish line.

Before you start reading, spend some time in prayer for yourself and the others in your group.

While You Read

As you read each chapter, use these pages to take notes, make outlines, highlight definitions, or write out what is confusing to you or why you disagree with me. There are no right or wrong answers here.

Keep in mind that reading the content and taking a few notes beforehand is a great way to prepare some thoughts for your study group. Maybe someone else needs to ponder your question or hear your insight—you're not just doing this for yourself.

So, while you read each chapter, I want you to use this study guide to do these three things:

1. Note any scripture passages that stand out to you.
2. Write out thoughts or copy phrases that connect dots for you or spark wonder, confusion, anger, or disagreement.
3. Summarize your experience, questions, or insights about the chapter in the "I want to remember . . ." section—the one thing you want to bring up to your group.

Chapter 25

Pregnant with a Prophet

Perhaps the most shocking place that I've seen this myth appear is on the lips of Jesus of Nazareth as He's debating some Pharisees in Matthew's gospel. (page 227)

Scripture in This Chapter

Matthew 12:39–40

Jonah 1:17

Proverbs 25:2

Jonah 1:4–5, 11–13

Jonah 2:5–6

Jonah 2:2

Thoughts, Insights, Questions

_____

_____

_____

_____

_____

I want to remember . . .

_____

_____

_____

Chapter 26

The Genesis of Jesus

John starts his gospel account with some iconic words: "In the beginning" (1:1).

In. The. Beginning. Talk about bold.

John is making it very clear right away that he is writing a new Genesis. (page 233)

Scripture in This Chapter

John 1:1

Genesis 2:1–2

John 19:30

John 20:1

Romans 8:11

Thoughts, Insights, Questions

_____

_____

_____

_____

_____

I want to remember . . .

_____

_____

_____

Chapter 27

The Jesus That John Knew

The first clue that jumps off the pages is the overwhelming presence of water in John's gospel. There's water everywhere—which should immediately cause our internal alarms to go off because water is our primary symbol for Chaos and creation. (page 239)

Scripture in This Chapter

John 20:21–22   John 4:46–53
Genesis 2:7

Thoughts, Insights, Questions

_____

_____

_____

_____

_____

I want to remember . . .

_____

_____

_____

Chapter 28

The Jesus Judas Thought He Knew

If John were to place a story in his gospel to
demonstrate Jesus passing the test of a lifetime,
where would that test take place? Probably a
garden, right? (page 246)

Scripture in This Chapter

John 18:3

Matthew 16:21–28

Matthew 20:17–19

Matthew 26:1–2

Mark 8:31–38

Mark 9:9–12, 30–32

Mark 10:32–45

Luke 9:43–45

Luke 18:31–34

John 18:10

Matthew 27:3–5

1 Corinthians 6:19

Thoughts, Insights, Questions

_____

_____

_____

_____

_____

I want to remember . . .

_____

_____

_____

Chapter 29

The Chaos Crusher

Jesus was undefeated against Chaos in the Gospels. Every single piece of evidence pointed to the fact that Jesus of Nazareth would continue an undefeated streak of crushing Chaos, but then the chaos of death defeated Jesus on the cross. (page 255)

Scripture in This Chapter

Luke 23:44–45

Matthew 27:50–51

1 Corinthians 2:8

John 12:24–25

John 11:4, 21, 32

John 20:14–15

Genesis 3:24

Genesis 2:8

Thoughts, Insights, Questions

_____

_____

_____

_____

_____

I want to remember . . .

_____

_____

_____

After You Read

Flip back to the "Before You Read" section. Did anything from the book or from the scriptures referenced address any plot holes you described? Think through any new understanding here.

_____

_____

_____

_____

_____

Look back at your chapter notes, and gather everything you wrote after "I want to remember . . ." here in this space. These are the thoughts and questions you want to bring to your group.

_____

_____

_____

_____

_____

_____

_____

_____

_____

_____

_____

_____

_____

_____

Take a moment now to say a prayer for your group before you gather, asking the Holy Spirit to guide the conversation. Flip back to the space where you wrote every person's name so you can pray for them personally.

SESSION 6

THE PRINCE OF PEACE: SECOND HALF

All Together

Opening Prayer (5 min.)

Begin your time in prayer, asking God to join you during this time of study.

Overview of Scripture and Content from *Crushing Chaos* (10 min.)

Take turns reading the scriptures referenced below and the related passages from the book. Try to give every person in the group a chance to look up a scripture passage or read the given chapter excerpt.

Matthew 12:39–40

Jonah sinks to the bottom of the *tehom*. Is swallowed up by Chaos. Calls the belly of the beast the realm of the dead—aka his tomb.

But then the belly of the beast is revealed to be a womb instead of a tomb.

And thus, Jonah is reborn.

This is what Jesus saw. This is what Matthew 12 is about.

Which is why He used this story to predict that His tomb would also be a womb—and that from His resurrection, new-creation life would enter the world. (From chapter 25: Pregnant with a Prophet)

John 20:1

Paul says in his letter to the Romans that "the Spirit of him who raised Jesus from the dead is living in you" (8:11). The Resurrection proves that the animating power of the Holy Spirit can accomplish what is absolutely impossible with mere human power and means. The Resurrection proves that a new day has dawned and that humanity has crossed into a new creation world where the Holy Spirit is available in a new way.

And now that the Holy Spirit dwells in us, we can finally get to the sixth and final stage of the Chaos cycle and demonstrate to the Lord that we can be tested and trusted. The resurrection of Jesus means the rules on the playing field have permanently changed. (From chapter 26: The Genesis of Jesus)

John 4:49–50

John intentionally portrays Jesus in a way that forces his audience to realize that a new creation is now at work within this old creation and that we have to choose to engage in the creation we discern spiritually as well as the one we experience with our physical senses. (From chapter 27: The Jesus That John Knew)

Luke 18:31–34

In Eden, the Dragon promised that Adam and Eve would be like God once they ate the fruit, but the reality is that they were already like God. They had been made in His image. In Gethsemane, the Dragon tries to convince Jesus that He can rescue Israel another way, without the excruciating pain of the Cross. Judas's way is a viable option. But this temptation fails. Jesus knows exactly who He is, and the river of behavior always flows from the lake of identity. (From chapter 28: The Jesus Judas Thought He Knew)

John 12:24–25

That's the gospel. God planted a garden. Chaos replaced it with a wilderness. For three years of earthly ministry, Jesus worked tirelessly to landscape His Father's vineyard and restore the Order that had been lost and nearly forgotten. Then in a shocking turn of events, Chaos defeated the second Adam, the Gardener, on the cross as darkness and death prevailed. But in killing Jesus, Chaos planted the seed of new creation into the soil of this earth. (From chapter 29: The Chaos Crusher)

Our Questions (20–30 min.)

Flip back to the "After You Read" portion of this session. What questions, thoughts, and insights do you have for one another? Was anything confusing or particularly illuminating?

Explore the following questions if you have time. You don't have to go in order—stick with the questions that sound interesting and cover new ground in your discussion.

- What kinds of reactions have you seen—or had—in response to inconsistencies in the Scriptures? What does Manny offer as one purpose of these kinds of inconsistencies, and how does his explanation sit with you?
- What is the sign of Jonah that Jesus speaks about in Matthew 12:39–40? Why is it important?
- Name a few ways that John shows his gospel to be a reinterpretation of Genesis.
- Pinpoint the moment of restart in John's gospel. What does Jesus say, and what's the link to Genesis?
- In Genesis 2 and John 20, we watch as God breathes on His people. What's the significance of the link?
- The words of Jesus have the power to bring order to our lives—but what is our part in it? How do we often resist Him?
- What's the significance of the number seven in the gospel of John?
- Why did the disciples struggle so much with the idea of a suffering Messiah?
- Describe how you reacted to Manny's interpretation of the character of Judas Iscariot.
- How was the Crucifixion a mistake on the part of the Dragon?
- How do we reconcile the realities of death and pain with Jesus's promise to us? Here's a place to start: Jesus never said, "Lazarus won't die." He said, "This sickness will not end in death."
- What's the symbolic importance of gardens in the Bible? What human ability is on display in a garden that contrasts with the wilderness?

In My Life (10 min.)

What is one thing you've learned or understood over the course of this study that changed your perspective on Christ? How would you explain it to a friend?

Try to give each person in the group who wants to share a minute or two to do so.

Closing Prayer (5 min.)

Close in prayer, thanking God for one another and the weeks you've spent together.

© ANDREW CHEW

MANNY ARANGO is a Bible nerd and founder of ARMA Courses—an online educational platform that helps Christians become biblically literate. The platform has grown to thousands of monthly subscribers since launching in 2020.

Born in Boston, Massachusetts, Manny was a teaching pastor at Social Dallas under pastors Robert and Taylor Madu, and is now the lead pastor, along with his wife, Tia, of The Garden in Houston, Texas. He graduated from Northern Seminary in June 2024 with a doctorate in New Testament studies.

Manny has been married to his beautiful wife for more than a decade, and they have a son named Theophilus.

Instagram: @mannyarango

TikTok: @manny_arango

Also from author and pastor
MANNY ARANGO

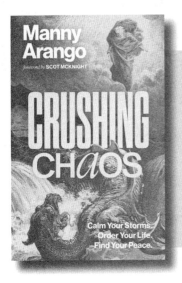

A deeply biblical and fresh look at how an ancient reading of the Bible leads to lasting peace, inviting followers of Jesus to join Him in bringing order to the chaos of their lives and the world.

In this compelling companion guide to the book *Crushing Chaos*, engage with key questions, dig into the Bible, and complete activities that will help you chart a path through the chaos to a life of order, joy, and peace.

WATERBROOK

Learn more about Manny Arango's books at
waterbrookmultnomah.com.